Minimalist Budget

*Everything You Need To Know About
Saving Money, Spending Less And
Decluttering Your Finances With Smart
Money Management Strategies*

Mary Connor

Copyright 2018 © Mary Connor

Legal & Disclaimer

The following document is reproduced below with the goal of providing information that is as accurate and reliable as possible.

This declaration is deemed fair and valid by both the American Bar Association and the Committee of Publishers Association and is legally binding throughout the United States.

Furthermore, the transmission, duplication or reproduction of any of the following work including specific information will be considered an illegal act irrespective of if it is done electronically or in print. This extends to creating a secondary or tertiary copy of the work or a recorded copy and is only allowed with an express written consent from the Publisher. All additional right reserved.

The information in the following pages is broadly considered to be a truthful and accurate account of facts, and as such any inattention, use or misuse of the information in question by the reader will render any resulting actions solely under their purview. There are no scenarios in which the publisher or the original author of this work can be in any fashion deemed liable for any hardship or damages that may befall them after undertaking information described herein.

Additionally, the information in the following pages is intended only for informational purposes and should thus be thought of as universal. As befitting its nature, it is presented without assurance regarding its prolonged validity or interim quality. Trademarks that are mentioned are done without written consent and can in no way be considered an endorsement from the trademark holder.

Table of Contents

Introduction

M any people have considered going on a budget. They want to be able to reign in their finances, but they worry that it is going to be too hard or that it will take them too long to accomplish. They don't think they can accomplish their goals or they are worried that they are going to feel too deprived and they just want to give up before they get started.

With minimalism budgeting, you will learn that there is another way. There are a lot of different budgeting plans out there, ones that promise to get you out of debt, but then the steps they offer make you feel guilty if you ever go out to eat or have any fun. Sure, you can get out of debt with those issues, but you are not living your best life and you probably aren't happy in the process, and this simply leads you to feel very deprived.

In this guidebook, we are going to take a look at a different approach to budgeting. Sure, we will discuss a bunch of budgeting methods that you can try out to fit your style and your personal preferences, but we are going to concentrate more on why budgeting as a minimalist is such a good idea.

In the past, when you looked at budgeting, you probably concentrated on how much you could deprive yourself to get those bills paid off. But this way of looking at things can be boring, difficult, and just no fun at all. But with minimalism budgeting, you learn that it is not about being miserable. It is about spending your money on things that you really love in life and eliminating all the waste and unnecessary purchases.

How many times have you gone out and

purchased a product because of advertising or because someone else recommended it, without actually needing the product? How many times have you spent too much on Christmas and birthdays and gone into debt? How much of your income are you paying to your debts each month? And are any of these purchases or spending habits making you feel happy?

When you learn how to create a budget that plays towards your goals and your passions in life, things begin to change. You stop overspending at Christmas. You only purchase an item if it helps you meet your goals and if you really need it. And this can be so empowering. It can feel great to not have a lot of clutter around your home, to not have to worry about paying off debts for things that bring you no happiness.

This can take time. We have been conditioned to spend a lot of money, even if it is on things that we don't need. Companies and advertisers have spent a lot of money and time learning how to do this. But with the help of this guidebook, and many of the topics and budgeting techniques that we will discuss in this guidebook, you can learn to only purchase the things that hold some value to you. It may take some time, and some months may not work as well as others, but over time, you will be able to cut down on your expenses and your debts and see the financial goals that you only dreamt about in the past.

Chapter 1:
Why is Budgeting So Important?

udgeting is a word that many of us have heard before, but we may have different definitions associated with it. According to the Business Dictionary, budgeting is an estimate of resources, revenues, and costs over a specified period, such as a month or a year, that will reflect a reading of future financial conditions and goals. This is kind of convoluted definition, but budgeting is going to be a method of making a plan on how you want to spend your money. When you create this kind of spending plan, you help yourself foresee whether or not you are going to have enough money to purchase the things that you need, and some of the things that you like.

Each person is going to create a budget that works the best for them. There is some flexibility in how you create your own budget. Many people choose to work on a budget to help them prioritize their spending to help them save money for each consecutive month. Slowly, by focusing on saving your money to purchase the things that you need or the ones that you need, it becomes easier to get these items without entering into more debt.

Many of us assume that we just need to make

more money in order to deal with the bills that pile up. But often, we just need to set up a budget and follow it, and we can do very well on less. If you have a goal set to save more money, then with the right budgeting tool, you will be able to put some of your money away each month. Even if it is just five percent of your income, that is a good start to your savings plan.

Since budgeting helps to give you some transparency with your finances, it helps you to have enough money for your needs, and maybe even some of your wishes. If you commit to following the budget that you set, and you learn that you don't need to always keep up with the neighbors all the time, you are going to find that there may actually be some extra money at the end of the month while paying off debts. Many people have debts to handle when they get started with budgeting. This plan can ensure that you can slowly work your way out of the debt without accumulating more

In addition to helping you manage the money that you have and get rid of debt, budgeting can also take some of the stress out of your life. Some people just let their money flow in and out without any plan. But then they are stressed out each month without having any idea of how much money they have and if they will actually have enough to get through the month. Staying financially unaware of where you are is not the best approach to life.

Being financially aware may make you feel worried in the beginning, but that is because you started out with no idea where your finances were. Once you get a budget down and you know where all of your money is, then life can become less stressful you will know exactly where your money is, where it is going, and what you will do with it. Being financially aware is part of being an adult and being responsible with the money can make all the difference in your life. It may seem scary at first, and many of us don't want to face where our finances are. This guidebook aims to help make some differences in the way you spend your money so you can actually control your finances and get those debts paid down.

What is budget planning and forecasting?

When you first work on creating a spending plan and using it, you are going to see how transparent your life is. you will be able to see what you spend your money on each day. This look can provide you with some insights on how you spend your money and some of the changes that you can make to cut more expenses if needed. When you get familiar with what it means to live within your means and on your budget, it becomes easier for you to map out your finances six months or more in advance.

This process is known as budget planning

Budget planning is nice because it helps you consider all the income and the expenses that you plan to have over the next few months. If you want to make one of these, get a calendar or another planning tool and write down everything in your budget for each month that you want to plan. This helps you to get a forecast on which months will have extra money that you can put into savings or put towards debts, and the months that you may need to tighten up the budget a bit more.

For example, you may look at your budget plan and see that you have your spouse's and your child's birthday in April. This is the month where you will need to spend a bit extra to pay for the presents. But in March, your month is pretty free and you don't have any extras to spend on. You can take some of the money that is extra in

March and use it to spend on those presents in April without harming your budget at all. This process, basically, is budget forecasting.

In most cases, the expenses that you have from one month to another won't be linear. You need to be able to think ahead, forecast what is going to happen, and then plan out your budget to even out the lows and the highs of your finances. There are going to be months when you have more expenses than others, and forecasting is going to help you plan out for each of them.

Making a budget plan ahead from three to six, and even twelve months in the future can help you forecast a lot of things. It helps you plan out your emergency savings, high-cost needs such as a car or house, and money to pay for vacations while also paying the regular bills that you have. When you decide to make these plans, you need to be realistic and honest with yourself. If you have an income that is on the lower side, it won't be a good idea to work towards saving an amount that is fifty percent of your income.

However, this budget plan is going to help you clearly see where your income is right now. You may find that it doesn't reasonably allow you to live the lifestyle that you want, even if you go crazy with saving and tighten your belt. A budget can reveal a lot about your finances and can sometimes be the motivation that you need to change jobs to make more, to improve your savings plan, and make changes that get you in the financial position that you want.

How is budgeting going to help my life?

Budgeting can be a great way to help you learn how to better manage your finances, and in the beginning, it will help you to find and highlight some of your bad spending habits. When you create a budget, you can see the whole numbers that you are dealing with, and sugar coating the problem isn't an option. Building a solid budget is a great way to notice the items that you don't need so you cut them out and won't waste money on them.

Here, we are talking more about the hidden things. We are talking about having the largest cable package when you only watch a few channels or you rather watch Netflix or other shoes online. We are talking about purchasing another purse even though your closet is full of them at home. With a good and honest budget, you are going to see that these useless expenses may make you feel good in the morning, but they are the reason that you can't put money into savings, that you can't go on vacation, or you have to purchase the cheapest food.

If you are thinking about creating a budget and

you notice that your current salary doesn't seem to cover the compulsory bills, then you can either look through the budget and figure out what you are able to cut, or you need to learn how to make more money. Since there are only so many hours in the day, and you often want to have time for sleep, spending with family, and doing other things you enjoy, downsizing is often easier. You need to find those extra expenses that you are able to cut out to make your current income go further.

The other benefit that you are going to receive when you decide to get started with budgeting is that it can do some wonders for helping you prepare for life events that you don't expect. These can be positive or negative, but they are things that pop up and you didn't plan for ahead of time. Without a budget, you likely have zero in savings and you will be stressed out worrying about how you will pay for it. Emergencies are never going to happen at the right time and creating a budget that includes some savings can make these situations easier to handle.

The benefits of creating a budget

There are so many benefits that can come into your life when you choose to add in a budget. It can take some time, and it does mean that you have to say no more often than you did in the past. But the amount of freedom that you will be able to gain when you no longer have to pay off objects that you don't need and that don't bring you any happiness, can really be worth it all. Add to that the amount of time that you can free up when you no longer have to pick up, maintain, or clean that item, and budgeting can quickly become your best tool when living a minimalistic lifestyle. Some of the benefits that you can see when you decide to start budgeting your money include:

- Can give you more control over your money: A budget is a good way to start adding some intention to the way that you save and spend your money. If you don't have a budget, your money is going to start controlling you. Budgeting can help you reduce stress when you don't have to make sudden adjustments because of lack of planning and it helps you to think and plan for some of your long-term goals.

- Keeps you focused on any financial goals that you have. Once you have some financial goals in place, you will find that it is easier to avoid unnecessary spending on anything that isn't going to contribute to those goals.

- Helps you be aware of what is going on with your money: When you create a budget, you are going to have a clearer picture of what money comes into your account, how quickly you are going to use it, and where that money is going. A budget can let you know what you are able to afford and can even help you to lower your debt. There is just so much that you can learn about your income, your spending, and all your finances.

- Helps you to get started with some savings: Many people have nothing put into savings because they assume they don't earn enough. But if you spent any time concentrating on creating a budget, you would be surprised at how a few changes in your spending could actually help you put quite a bit into savings.

- Helps you to be more prepared for unexpected things that may come up: Whether it is a trip to see a sick family member, a broken car, or a medical bill, a budget can help you prepare for when things don't quite go the way that you had expected.

- Helps you to take care of any debt that you have in a more efficient manner. No one wants to deal with debt, but you need to deal with it and get rid of it as quickly as possible. A good budgeting plan can make this process so much easier than before and you may be surprised at how easily you can get rid of your debts with a good budget.

- Can help you decide how your money is going to work for you: Quit letting your money just flow out of your account without any idea of where it is going or how it is helping you to reach your own financial goals. With a good budget, you will have a better idea of how you are spending your money and where it is going. You can then choose where every dollar you end goes. Pick whether you want to spend it on something fun, on paying down more debt, put it into savings, or somewhere else that will benefit you the most.

- Can help you to get more money out of your income: With a good budget, you are better able to identify and then eliminate any spending that is unnecessary, such as interest, penalties, and late fees. These savings are going to really add up over time.

Can minimalism fit into my budget?

When you hear budget and minimalism, you probably think of someone who spends nothing, lives off Ramen noodles, and never goes out. It gives you images of a skinny budget that barely makes ends meet and forces you to really tighten the belt and be poor. But this is not really what a minimalist budget is about.

Even though you will need to make some changes to your current spending, this kind of budget isn't about purchasing as few things as possible, but more about having things that you truly love. So, instead of spending your money on a bunch of things you may never use, you learn how to save your money and spend it on things that truly give you some happiness. We will spend more time discussing this as we go through the rest of this guidebook.

Chapter 2:

What is Minimalism and How Can It Affect Your Budgeting?

Minimalism is a thought that many people don't fully understand. When they hear the words, they assume that it means they need to get rid of everything they own, only have one pair of clothes, never go on vacation, and basically never leave the house other than to go to work. They imagine someone who can't make ends meet at all and who is constantly struggling to get by.

This is not the way that minimalism works though. It is more about deciding what is really important for you and then spending your time and money on those things while getting rid of everything else. Many times in our modern culture, we fall into the trap of having to purchase more and more. We think that we need the newest gadget, the coolest toy, that we need to be out constantly spending our money. But all this leads us to is a ton of debt and things that we never even use in our lives.

With minimalism, you learn how to cut out some of the things that are unnecessary. You focus your time and energy on things that you really love. If you value going on a vacation but don't really care about going to the movies or on purchasing a lot of clothes, you would move to the minimum on those items and save up for some nicer vacations. If you really value books, you may keep many of these around, but then cut down on anything that doesn't bring you the same kind of joy.

Minimalism is not about getting rid of everything and living with nothing. It is more about bringing simplicity to your life, a simplicity that allows you to get more enjoyment out of life. In many cases, it can help you save money, but you are not required to cut out everything and live like a monk to make it happen. Just cut out the things that are just taking up space in your home, the things that don't even bring you joy. Fill that space with things that matter to you, things that bring you happiness, and you will see some great rewards.

Things you will notice when you become a minimalist

Adding a bit of minimalism to your life can make a big difference. You will notice that you spend less money. You will notice that life seems a bit easier and less stressful. You will find multiple uses for the same item and you won't spend as much time cleaning the items that you have sitting around the home. Some of the other things that you may notice changing in your life when you become a minimalist include:

- You may spend more time shopping, but purchase less: When you are a minimalist, you will take more time to make your buying decisions. In some cases, such as with a big purchase, you may think it over for a few months before you decide to make the purchase. When you go to the store, you will spend time researching the item to make sure that it does what you need or want.

- You can save money: Becoming a minimalist means that you can save money. You will stop giving in to your impulse purchases and only spend money on the things that matter to you the most. This, especially over time, can put more money into your pocket.

- You learn how to do without. As a minimalist, you will only keep around the things that you actually value or need. And you may use some things for more than one purpose. For example, canning jars can not only hold your canned goods, but work as organizers, food containers, and drinking glasses. The more uses that you can get out of an item, the more like a minimalist you are. As a minimalist, instead of heading to the store and purchasing something right away, you will see if there is anything around your home that you can use instead. This can help you save time, money, and clutter around the house.

- You gain more free time: When you reduce the amount of time that you spend purchasing new things, taking care of those items, organizing those items and looking for them when you need them again, you will be amazed at how much free time you gain. You can spend that doing a hobby, hanging out with friends and family, and doing things that you actually want to do.

- You know what you want to out of life: Each of the items that you place in your get-rid of pile as you declutter is a test of how well you know yourself. And when you go out and purchase a new item, you have to consider whether that item makes you happier and if it helps you to live the life that you really want.

Can minimalism help me budget better?

The idea of minimalism can definitely help you to create a more sound and better budgeting plan. You may even be surprised at how much less you can live on and not feel completely deprived when you begin with minimalism. Many people worry that they won't be able to come up with enough money to pay the bills each month. These are the same people who go out all the time, you purchase a bunch of clothes and purses and shoes that they never wear, and who don't pay any attention to what they spend their money on or even if they spend it on things that make them happy.

Despite what you may think about minimalism, it is not all about cutting your budget down to the bare bones and hoping that you can somehow make it on one meal a day and no new clothes or other items for the next ten years or more. It is more about being conscious about the spending decisions that you make. About thinking whether or not you actually need that item in your life or if you already have that item at home.

When we make more conscious decisions about what we want to spend our money on, and we take the right precautions to not fall prey to keeping up with others or all the advertising around us, it becomes easier to use our money wisely. And this is often what minimalist budgeting is about. It helps us to make smart spending decisions, ones that can actually make us happy and give us a fulfilling life, rather than wasting our money on items that we would never use and going deep into debt.

Chapter 3:
Traps of Minimalism

While we have spent some time talking about minimalism and all the benefits that come with it, there are a few things that you have to be aware of. It isn't always the best option and can lead to trouble if you don't use it wisely. Minimalism is a great method to help you truly enjoy life, but there has been a kind of distortion that comes with minimalism. For example, bloggers use it as a way to make money, companies will try to sell you products that you don't need in order to convince you that you are being a minimalism, and you may actually end up spending more time and money than you need, without actually getting any enjoyment out of it.

There are a variety of traps that you can fall into when you decide to implement a minimalistic budget and implement minimalism in your own life. Some of the traps that you should be careful about include:

The distortion of minimalism

In the new minimalism movement, not only fans are seeing a benefit, but so are service providers. Interior designers, restaurants, and furniture companies have seen this as an opportunity as well. These companies are sticking the word "minimalist" on some of their products and selling them at a much higher price point than their regular items. These items can end up costing you hundreds of thousands of dollars, even if you can find another similar product for less money and even if you don't need that item.

Even if you choose to go through and declutter

your home and live your life with much less, this doesn't mean that you automatically save money. It is possible to spend a ton of money each month and still be in the minimalist umbrella. For example, if you decide to finally add a dresser into your home, it isn't really saving you money if you spend $1000 just to get one that is considered minimalist.

This is all a big marketing ploy that is making some companies rich and making those who really want to save on their budget and become a minimalist very poor. Many of these consumers are looking to turn their lives around and do something good, but then they are tricked into getting these products, products that just cost them a lot of money and aren't really any better than regular, non-minimalistic, products.

The amount you spend can still be considered minimalism, but it could cost you a lot. knowing this, you need to be aware of the different traps that many sellers and companies are going to set for you. Being a minimalist is not all about picking out designer items that were labeled as minimal. You do not want to spend your whole income living in a minimalist environment minimalism can be done with regular objects that serve the purpose that you need, not by purchasing the most expensive item that you can find.

You don't need to get rid of everything

Many people who hear about minimalism assume that to follow this lifestyle, they need to throw everything away and only spend a few dollars a month on food. But this can be a miserable way to live life. It doesn't allow you to have any freedom, and you will feel really deprived in no time. Life as a minimalist is not supposed to be horrible, it is supposed to be stress free and full of many of the things that you enjoy and that make your life full.

There are many different ways that you can live a minimalist lifestyle. Some people spend their time going on trips. Some save up to purchase a home. Some like to just purchase a lot of good literature and fill up their time reading. There are different ways to do this lifestyle and none of them are wrong. As long as you figure out what is important to you and brings you passion in life, and you get rid of anything that doesn't fit into this ideal or into your perfect life, then you are following the minimalist lifestyle.

It is hard to know what you really value

The first step in this process is to figure out what you value and what you want out of life. What things do you want out of life? What brings you a lot of joy and happiness and what do you want to pursue more in your life? These are questions that you need to consider before you decide to get started with minimalism. If you have no idea what you value, it is really hard for you to know what needs to stick around or not with minimalism.

But figuring out what truly makes you happy in life can be hard. We have been hit with a lot of different advertisements in our lives, lots of messages from others, and many companies who want to convince us that we can only be happy with their product or what they are selling. It may take some time to figure out what is really important to us, what we really enjoy so that we can use that information to help us live a life of minimalism.

It can be hard to give up all the material possessions that you own

Many people find that it is hard to give up the material possessions that they own. They have attached some emotional value to these objects, and this can make it hard to get rid of the item. Even if there isn't a lot of value on that item, they may feel bad about all the money they put into that item, and they don't want to waste it. Minimalism doesn't expect you to get rid of everything that you own in order to get the benefits, but you do need to go through and decide what is valuable to you and what isn't, and then get rid of the things that aren't valuable to you. When you assign a value to all your items, it can be hard to get rid of a lot of the things in your home.

Can create a false sense of being deprived

Many people decide to start following minimalism and jump all in. they get all the bags and start throwing everything away or donating it. They make a pledge to never buy anything extra again and plan out their meals to purchase as little as possible. While this is a great way to save you money, if you go overboard with it all, you are going to feel deprived and unhappy with your decision very quickly.

It is not a good idea to jump into this process too quickly. If you get rid of most of the items that you own, you are going to feel deprived. Maybe decide to work on one room at a time and slowly get rid of items. You can always go back through and do it again if you decide. And always make sure that you know your passions and what you want out of life before starting. This will give you the motivation that you need and can ensure you keep the right things around when you start minimalism.

Other disadvantages of minimalism

There are a lot of great things that can come from following a minimalist lifestyle you can start to save money, you can enjoy more free time with those you love, and you can avoid purchasing things that you don't need and don't get any happiness from. But there can also be some issues with following a minimalist lifestyle. In addition to some of the issues that we talked about above, you must also be aware of include:

- You may miss out on the real meaning of minimalism and then go out of control you may get rid of too many things. This can leave you feeling deprived and dissatisfied with the new life.

- It is possible that your friends and family will find you weird.

- You may start to feel a bit conceited

because of this new lifestyle, which is not the point of it.

- You may become too fixated with making sure you never own more than a certain number of possessions rather than pursuing your passions with this lifestyle.

- You will spend the extra free time that you have in an unwise manner.

- Minimalism is going to take some discipline and even some strong mental health.

- It is not always easy to apply minimalism into your daily life.

The biggest thing to remember about becoming a minimalist is to not try to make all the changes overnight. You want to do this process gradually and find the right balance that can fit your situation and preferences.

If you feel like you are trapped in a world of consumerism and always being busy and you feel that you are overwhelmed, then it may be time to think about minimalism. It allows you to enjoy more out of your life, to find your passions, and to get out of the cycle of living paycheck to paycheck. It can sometimes be hard to accomplish, but if you slowly work towards it, it can help you reach the true freedom that you want in your life.

Chapter 4:
The Psychology of Purchasing

The way that we purchase things, and the reason, has been a topic of much debate. Many of us think that we are in control of the way we spend our money, that we can make unbiased decisions that serve our needs well. But then we look around our homes and see a ton of items that we have purchased (that come with a lot of debt), that we don't need and we realize the power of advertising and how convincing many big companies can be.

The psychology of purchasing can be a powerful tool and can give us some great insight into why we purchase the things that we do. Let's take a look at some of the studies that have been done on this topic and delve into some of the ways that you can gain more control over your purchases right from the start.

The Iowa gambling test

The first study we are going to look at is a famous one done by researchers from the University of Iowa. It was designed in order to simulate some real-life decision making that the participants would partake in.

In this study, the participants were shown four decks of cards. They were told that choosing some cards would give them money, and some cards would make them lose money. The aim here was to collect as much money out of your picks as possible. But what the participants didn't know was that the first two decks were ones that were considered bad decks and would lead them to long-term losses, and the other two decks were good decks, that would provide them long-term gains.

During this study, the researchers measured the

physiological measurements of all the participants while they were making choices. The data measurement showed that the participants were able to tell the losing or the winning quality of the decks after going through between forty and fifty cards. They could explain why picking cards from the last two decks was a much better idea. But the participants had different mental processes that were measured apart from the previous one.

The participants showed a stress response, including more sweat and higher skin conductivity, after they picked out just ten cards out of those bad decks. Subconsciously, they foresaw the punishment followed by the bad pick thirty or forty cards before they were able to logically explain it. Shortly, their subconscious mind was able to figure out the game long before they could consciously figure it out.

The human mind doesn't work on rational deliberation only. It is a mix up of rational and emotional decisions. Emotional responses are going to be very automatic and we often don't even notice they are happening because they are fueled by intuition. These types of responses move quickly and naturally, even if we don't have the information that is needed to come to a conclusion. And they are often subconsciously made.

On the other hand, rational answers are ones that are conscious. These are slower and will require more effort. Rational and logical responses are often harder to make, which is why many people will choose to rely on their intuition in most cases.

When it comes to decisions about purchasing something, buyers are going to be more inclined to take out their credit cards led by emotional processing. People are going to make their decisions based on how they feel or the associations that they come up with about the product, not on whether or not the object tin question is actually something that they need, or whether it is actually worth the price.

Sellers and many big companies are going to know this information and will try to take advantage of it. The biggest magician in the industry on selling a feeling is Apple. They are going to sell a perceived status of the product. Objectively thinking, some competitors could sell you a much higher quality of product for a lower price, giving you a better value. But Apple has done some great advertising that helps you to rely on them and makes it so that you are willing to purchase their product over others.

Rationality versus the emotions

When we look at the brain, there are two sides, the left, and the right hemisphere. The right side of your brain is the side that is artistic, subjective, and intuitive. The left is going to be the analytical and logical side. While all people are going to use both sides of the brain in some respect, there are some tests that can show you which one you tend to rely on the most. But even if you have a dominant side of the brain, it doesn't mean that the other side has no influence on the decisions that you make. This is especially true when it comes to your buying decisions. No one is able to base their purchases just on pure logic; there is often an element of feeling and emotion involved.

For example, when you want to purchase a new car, what would you pick out based on just logic. With this idea, you would pick out the safest and cheapest option, something that has a lot of security and something that takes them from A to B. Yet, there are some people who will still buy the Bugatti. There are plenty of cheaper and safer cars out there and your logical state is going to tell you to pick one type of car. But your emotional mind is going to get you to pick things like color, status, and horsepower instead. If you pick the Bugatti in this situation, the brain has conspired against you and your budget.

When you make a purchase of something due to smart rationalizing, we are going to think that our decision for that purchase is well founded. We will imagine ourselves with all the benefits that we think this object will give you. We like to fantasize about the gains and all the benefits that you are able to get for the purchase. Sellers know that you will feel this way, and they know exactly how to stroke your ego with the items that they are going to sell you.

The seller is often so good at doing this that they can convince you that you are making a logical decision, when in fact they have brought out your emotional side and are trying to get that side of the brain to make a decision. They will give a short presentation about the product and will highlight all the benefits you will get from the product as a buyer. They will use words like never, always, the best, the only, the XY product for smart, conscious, stylish people, and more.

Through this work, you will start to feel obliged to purchase that product. If you don't, you may feel that you are not conscious, smart, and or stylish. You can simply purchase this product to get those feelings in your life.

However, the best marketing strategies are not focused on future benefits. They are going to state that your product is able to offer an easy and quick solution to your pain points. Why do companies do this? It is much easier for the company to relate to your current pain point, or your current state, rather than trying to imagine a yet nonexistent future happiness.

Stating that someone is no longer going to suffer is a much more powerful motivation to purchase a product. Once the customer has the conviction that the seller understands their current problem and is able to fix it, the chances that they are going to purchase it is higher. An example of this is that you are more eager to purchase a product that promises to make your acne go away in just two days compared to one that promises to make your skin look flawless at a future date.

Another word that you need to watch out for when you hear advertising and marketing is the word "sale". Our left brain will get shot down and then imprisoned when you see that word. The emotional side will fall in love with the item and it will shoot down the left brain by saying "Look, the item is a discount so it makes sense now to get the item." It takes a lot of work and willpower to convince yourself that the item isn't something you need and you may make the purchase.

This works really well for advertisers because they can get a lot of people to agree to purchase the item. But it doesn't work well for you and for your new minimalist budget. You are likely to fall for these mind traps, without even realizing what is going on. And this can get you in a trap of too many items all over the place, items that you don't really need.

The reciprocity principle

When we get something from someone, we feel a sense of obligation to pay back what we received.

This is known as the reciprocity principle and it does a good job of explaining why free gifts to customers and others can be so effective. For example, there is a soap company that is popular in Europe who has a marketing strategy where an attractive boy or girl will distribute free samples of soap close to the store. These sales people are able to hook the customers with this free gift and can often get the customer to try out samples and purchase the product better than any other marketing tool.

To make you feel indebted to them, the seller doesn't even have to provide a gift that is expensive. It can be something like information or a smaller piece of a larger product that you may then be tempted to purchase. The secret here is that sellers are going to give you something for free. This makes you feel indebted to them a bit and can help build up some trust and good will with that person. You are then more likely to want to return the favor and purchase that item from them.

If you are working on creating a minimalist budget, then you need to watch out for this kind of idea. You are allowed to take the free sample if you want to try it out, but that does not mean that you are obligated to actually purchase the product. Take a look around your home and think about how many items that you have purchased because the company offered you a free gift or something else in the process. This is just wasting a lot of your time and money and cluttering up your home at the same time. If you are too tempted by the free samples, then just refuse to take them in the first place.

The social proof

This is a principle that lays on the idea that you trust more of what other people endorse than things that are not. We are more inclined to go after a product that has an endorsement that we trust. For example, we may choose to purchase cooking equipment if Gordon Ramsey is selling it than when there is no endorsement at all. If we do any online shopping, we tend to purchase stuff that has more customer reviews, and things with a four star rating, rather than other products.

Commitment and consistency

The best new customer to a business is an old customer. This is the golden truth of marketing. It is a lot easier to convince one of your existing customers to purchase another product from your store rather than bringing in a new customer. This is why sellers have a specific strategy of how to keep people hooked to the store after their first purchase. And many buyers are happy to shop at a store they trust and get a nice discount at the same time.

Many customers are going to be rewarded for their loyalty to a particular company. But just because you have shopped at a store in the past doesn't mean that you have to shop there every time that they send you a coupon. There is nothing wrong with shopping there again if you actually need one of the products, but you need to make that decision consciously rather than becoming a constant shopper of things that you don't need just because they hand you a coupon or provide you with an incentive.

Scarcity

Many customers are really attracted to items that are considered rare or unique. Purchasing and then owning these items can make them feel special. In economic theory, this scarcity is going to relate to demand and supply. The higher the demand for the item, the more expensive it is. this is because more people want it than there are items to purchase. This means that the people who get the item are going to need to pay a higher price to get it. If there is less of something, the more valuable it becomes to people.

In most cases, when an advertiser decides to make something seem scarce, there really isn't a worry of scarcity. This is just some good sellers who are working hard to make us believe that it is. For example, some planes may convince you that there are only three seats available on that flight. This makes it seem like you need to make the purchase right then and there so they can fill it up. But if you watch the seats for a few weeks, those three seats will all magically still be available. The idea was to present the idea of scarcity to you for those seats so that you would be more likely to purchase them.

Be careful of your online purchases

When you take your time to when doing an online purchase, you will be less likely to make an impulse purchase. Researchers conclude that non-purchasers and purchasers on almost all websites showed the same pattern of behavior. Those who made the purchase often spent a lot less time on the webpage compared to those who decided not to purchase it. The purchasers were less likely to read through the details and were less distracted by the information that was shared about the product.

What this can mean is that if you feel that you have a bad shopping urge when you go online and you want to work on your budget, you must make sure that you do the opposite of what marketers want for you to do when you shop online. You should take the time to read the details, the reviews, the specification and everything about the product that you can. Then take the time to compare them with other similar products and notice how they compare. What this does is put you in an analysis paralysis and you may lose your appetite for binge shopping faster than usual.

Marketers have spent a lot of time learning how best to take away the money that is in your budget. You may start out with the best intentions of doing minimalism, but these marketers are skilled at trying to take your money away from you. Being away of some of the techniques that you see and making sure that you avoid falling for them can make a big difference in how many unnecessary items you purchase and how well you are able to keep yourself on a budget.

Chapter 5:
How to Get over Some of Your Compulsive Spending Habits

N ow that we know a little bit about how our minds work when it comes to purchasing something, it is time to learn some of the basics of how to get over your compulsive spending habits. If you work on adding minimalism in your lifestyle, it isn't going to do you a lot of good to then go out and give in to a lot of compulsive purchases at the same time. Learning how to tame these compulsive spending habits can go a long way in helping you to keep on budget and avoid issues with more clutter in your life.

What is compulsive spending?

A compulsive buying disorder is an obsessive shopping habit that can bring about adverse consequences to the person who does it. It can also be seen as an irresistible and uncontrollable urge resulting in excessive, expensive, and time-consuming retail activity that can be prompted and brought on by a negative activity. It can also result in gross personal, financial, and social difficulties.

Compulsive buying disorder can be triggered by a ton of different things, such as the desire to be accepted by others, perfectionism, the need to have control or just a general impulsiveness in the person. It can also be an issue with the manifestation of identity, social position, anxiety, depression, low self-confidence, and more. Of course, not all of these are going to apply in every case, but often one or more will be the underlying cause.

Now, for those who are wealthy, this disorder can seem like a regular pastime. But for those who are on a tight budget and who are living paycheck to paycheck, this is a condition that could ruin their lives. Those who are dealing with this condition and need to budget must come up with a plan to help them out.

The difference between the regular shopping that

most people do, and between CBD is the compulsive and overwhelming desire to buy and spend money against the better judgment or the negative consequences that can come from it. Non-addicted buyers will make a purchase because of utility and for real need. But those who are compulsive buyers are going to purchase in order to balance their emotions and improve their mood.

Just like with any other addiction, this buying disorder is going to have roots in a dissatisfied emotional need. Since we know that ads are in charge of triggering the emotions, it is not hard to figure out how this can affect a person who craves satisfying that need. It is going to feel like a drug to them. It can help provide them with a bit of relief when that purchase is able to satisfy the need, but it won't take time for those positive effects to fade. They will then have a new and bigger dose later on.

How to overcome compulsive buying

If you want to follow a minimalistic budget, you need to make sure that you cut out any issues that you have with compulsive buying. This is going to get you into a trap of spending way too much money on items that you don't even need. Learning how to overcome this compulsive buying can make a big difference in following a minimalistic lifestyle.

The quickest way for you to overcome this issue is to raise better emotional awareness. If the problem is really severe for you, then it may be a good idea to talk with a therapist and discuss the underlying issue that is causing an issue. A professional is able to help you deal with healthy emotion regulation strategies to give you the help that you need to deal with these compulsive tendencies and then stop the mindless buying in the future.

You may also want to stick away from as much advertising as possible. Since this advertising is all over the place, it can be hard to deal with this and completely avoid the advertisements around us, but you can make a few changes, including looking online, on television, and even in the newspapers. If you aren't able to control your emotional attachment to the items you purchase, then it is best to avoid seeing the advertisements that will push you towards making those purchases in the first place.

Chapter 6:
How to Start a Minimalist Budget

N ow that we have spent some time talking about minimalism and all the parts that go with it, and we know some of the benefits that come with this kind of lifestyle and budget, it is time to talk about the steps you need to take to start your own minimalist budget. It isn't as difficult as you may think. And it really won't take much more time or effort than doing a regular budget. So, let's get started!

Change the mindset you have from borrowing and making payments, to owning the item

The first thing we need to take a look at is changing the way that our minds work. In many cases, we think of owning things in a way that just isn't true, and this can cause us a lot of issues down the road. It allows us to live above our means and can make it very difficult to get true happiness in any form.

Many times, people who are in a lot of debt or

who are broke will talk about owning things in terms of the payments that they make. They may say things like "I bought this car because I got a great deal on the lease – the payments are only $200 a month." The goal with this kind of mindset is to stretch out the finances as much as possible, helping the individual to get the lowest payments. This may allow them to live beyond their means using a certain lifestyle, but they can't really afford to do this.

With a minimalist budget, you need to flip this mindset around. Instead of thinking in terms of payments, you must think about things in terms of ownership. Don't spend time asking what the monthly payment is. instead, focus on what the actual cost of the item is, the amount that you would pay if you handed the money over right now, and then make the decision about whether you actually want to purchase it or not.

If you already have things that are on payment, work to get them paid off as quickly as possible. If you are looking to purchase something new in the future, then make sure that you pay for it in full, or save up to do this, rather than wasting all that money on interest that just makes someone else rich.

Define the values you have financially and then establish priorities

Now it is time to work on defining what your financial values are and establishing some of your financial priorities. In order to help you cut some of the unnecessary things out of your life, you need to figure out your financial values. This helps you to figure out what is considered unnecessary spending for you. If you value spending some time in the morning with friends at the local coffee shop, then go ahead and keep that in your budget. But if you just do it for a quick jolt of energy in the morning, then consider making coffee at home for example.

In this step, you must take the time to define what is necessary, or the most valuable, to you and your life. Once you know what your personal values are, it becomes easier to establish your financial priorities. Some of the things that you can write down as financial values will include:

- Retiring at the age of 60

- Donating 10 percent of your income to your church

- Have a 30 percent buffer between your expenses and your income

- Save 20 percent of your income for things you want or to have a buffer

- Live a life that is free of debt.

Once you have a clear picture of your financial values, you will then be able to take this information and establish your financial priorities. These priorities are basically going to be the goals that you have for your finances. They are the plan that you will make to get from where you are right now to where you want to be in the future.

There are many different financial priorities that you can make in your life. Some examples of the financial priorities that you may want to start planning may include:

- Create a financial plan for the long-term that can allow you to retire at age 55.

- Make 20 percent more income by starting a side job or finding a new job.

- After you pay off all of your debt, begin saving about 20 percent of your income.

- Pay off all your debt in three years. This can include debts like auto loans, student loans, and credit cards.

These are a few of the examples that you can look at when it comes to setting your financial priorities. There are so many different ways that you can work on creating your financial priorities. If you sit down and are unsure of what you should make your financials values or which priorities to set, you can work with the 50/20/30 budget. With this budget, you are going to set aside 50 percent of your budget to your needs, 20 percent to your savings and debts, and 30 percent to your wants.

Another item that you can consider is the value of experiences when they are compared to things. What research shows is that you are going to feel much happier when you spend money on experiences rather than spending them on things. Many times it feels like purchasing things can be the big key to happiness that we need, especially in traditional American culture. However, this isn't true and can usually lead us to feeling down and in debt.

This step should take up some time in your budgeting plan. It is so important that you take the time to establish your financial values and then define your priorities to help you create the perfect minimalist budget. Remember that the heart of minimalism is to prioritize the things that you see as the most important and then forgetting everything else. But you can't do this if you haven't decided what is most important to you.

Make a list of the way you spend your money now and then evaluate that consumption

The next step is to create a list of everything that you already spend your money on. This can include all your bills and housing payments as well as wedding expenses, travel, gifts, and everything else that your money goes to. It is important to make this list as detailed as you possibly can because this helps you get better results.

Once you have this list created, it is time to evaluate each thing on it. Ask yourself if each line item is something that you hold meaningful to your life or do you value it. Or, does that item help serve your financial values and priorities? If you say yes to one thing on the list, then you will have to say no to another because you don't have unlimited money to make it happen. And if you end up saying yes to something that doesn't really serve you, you will end up saying no to yourself in the long run.

Let's take a look at an example of this. You spend $150 a month on your hair. You write that down on the list and then ask if spending this amount is helping you to reach your financial goals. Yes, it may make you feel good, but you could probably cut the visits down a bit, or use some different products, and you won't really notice the difference.

If you take a look at that list and notice that you spend a lot of money on items that don't really fit in line with your financial priorities and values, then it is time to cut out these expenses from your minimalist budget. This doesn't mean that you can never spend money on them. It is fine to go get your hair done occasionally. But maybe learn how you can do some of the work at home on your own, and then go to the hair stylist a few times a year instead of a few times a month.

Find ways to simplify your credit cards and accounts

A minimalist budget is one that has one savings account and one checking account. Your checking account is the one that you need to use for all of your discretionary and non-discretionary expenses. This would include things such as entertainment, clothing, and other extra stuff along with bills, debt, and housing. The savings account is what should be used for saving up for a big vacation or as your emergency fund.

Another thing to consider is only having one credit card, even though some people consider not having any credit cards at all. This may mean that you have to give up some of your rewards, but you really will simplify your life and can make it easier to keep organized when it comes to your spending.

This is a big area that budgeters will make a mistake with. They will have a ton of savings and checking accounts. They may do this to help them save up for all the different goals that they have. For example, they may have an account for an emergency fund, one for a down payment on a house, one for taxes, one for vacation, and so on for all their goals. This method can be messy and you may even fall into the trap of borrowing money from one account to help fund another. Keep your accounts to a minimum to ensure that you can actually save up and not come out with a mess.

Create a realistic spending plan using your income and expenses

While the whole point of this is to create a minimalist budget, we are going to spend some time listing out the specific items that you may have as expenses that go against your income. You can work on adopting the right mindset, setting goals, and making things easier, but this step is all about breaking down your expenses and mindset and then decide where you would like each dollar of your income should go.

Each budget is going to be a bit different and it will depend on your personal bills and your own situation. For example, if you don't have any kids at this time, then you won't need to add that into the mix. An example of how the expenses may look in your minimalist budget include:

- Rent and mortgage
- Groceries
- Utilities
- Transportation
- Personal care
- Kids
- Travel
- Giving
- Entertainment
- Professional services
- Miscellaneous

Make sure to list out all of the expenses that you personally have. Keep it as simple as possible though and consider which areas you are able to cut out each month. You can write all this down in a budget spreadsheet if you wish and then update it each month to help you keep track of all the money that you do spend during the month.

Automate the payments for your bills to make things easier

Because minimalism is all about embracing an easier and simple way of organizing your finances, it makes sense that you would automate all, or as many as possible, of your payments with this budget plan. Automate your savings, debt payments, and all bill payments that you can. This helps you to get the money to the right places without having to worry about it as much. There are some bills that aren't set up for this yet but do as many of them as possible.

Question all the purchases you make in the future

After you take the time to implement a new budget into your life, it is important that you maintain it. And one way to do this is to carefully evaluate all the purchases that you make starting now and into the future. Through budgeting, you will have a good idea of how you have habitually spent your money in the past. Now, with this step, you need to question all of the purchases that you plan to make in the future. When you want to purchase something, take a moment and ask if that purchase is really necessary.

If you are uncertain about whether a purchase is worth it or not, consider how much time you would have to work in order to pay for that item. It takes time for you to earn money for those purchases, so for every purchase, you want to make, ensure that it is worth the time that you spent earning that money.

Schedule some time to review your finances and check on the progress.

Creating the budget is not the final step. It is an important step and you should give it the time and attention it deserves. But you also must make sure that you pay attention to the budget and that you follow it as closely as possible as you go along. Then, at predetermined intervals, you need to set time aside to review your progress and see how close you are to reaching your goals.

There are times when things will change in your life, and the plan that you originally came up with will no longer work for your needs. You may get a new job, want to purchase a home, have a child, or have another big life event occur. The original plan may not be able to handle these changes, and this is why a systematic review on a regular basis can be so useful.

To help you review, evaluate, and then revise the budget to ensure that it keeps on working for you, set up a financial meeting with yourself. If you can, do this each month, but a few times a year can often suffice as well. This helps you to implement and make any changes to the budget that you need.

A minimalist budget is just one method that you can use to help see results when it comes to controlling your money and getting it to work for your needs. Many people have their own form of budgeting that seems to work the best for them, but this method allows you to really look at your current spending habits and helps you to make changes at any time that you need. A minimalist budget is a great way to finally take a good look at your finances and then determine the best way to get those finances back in line.

Chapter 7:
The 50/30/20 Method

W hile the minimalist budget that we talked about above can be a great option to work with, there are other budgeting methods that can work quite well too. At this point, you should know that budgeting is more than paying all your bills on time. It is more complex than that, it includes spending, saving forecasting, and planning. The first budgeting method that we are going to look at is known as the 50/30/20 method.

The numbers in this budgeting pan are going to symbolize proportions in your monthly spending. This is a guideline that was created and then developed by financial advisors and money masterminds to help you keep all of your spending and expenses on track. Regardless of which stage in life you are currently in, you will be able to benefit when you adopt this kind of budgeting system.

Let's delve a bit more into this one. With this rule, you will take 50 percent of your income and use it for the essentials that you need and the bills you have to pay, 30 percent for your personal expenses, and then the final 20 percent is for your savings. This helps you to divide up your income to get the most out of it you can.

Spending fifty percent of your income on the essentials may seem like a very high number to start with, but you need to consider what all goes into this. This number is going to include everything from your housing bills to what you eat in the morning, so it is a very accurate percentage, even if it does seem a little bit high in the beginning.

The costs in this first amount are the ones that you are not able to give up or run away from. Everyone is going to pay them in more or less the same percentage. You can always reduce the essential costs, but they can then pop out somewhere else. The most common expense that you will see in this category include transportation, utility bills, housing costs, and food. You may also include internet bills and phone under here because most of us will need to pay this every month. You can move them to personal expenses if you wish.

The personal category is going to be the deal breaker category in your budget. If you want to really be a minimalist, then you may be able to reduce this even more and add some of that percentage to your savings category. It is for some of the extras that you may need during the money. If you don't spend the whole 30 percent, then you are doing this budgeting method well and you shouldn't stress on this at all.

Some people are going to have low demands when they do the self-defining costs and they will be able to cut out a lot of it. Experts provide this percentage to personal needs because there are often a lot of non-essentials that you want. But if you are able to live your full life in a minimalistic manner for only ten percent of your income, then that is fine and you can move the leftover money to your savings or to another area.

There are a lot of different expenses that you are able to add to this personal category, but they are also easy to drop if you wish. You may want to include options like dining out, gym memberships, clothing, makeup, coffee breaks, and cable TV bills. Any extra luxury options that you add to the essentials should be considered a personal expense as well.

And then you have the third category. This is going to be your savings, or the get ahead category. Having these savings can provide you with a feeling of safety, something to fall back on. This amount is often going to vary depending on who you talk with. This method asks you to save back 20 percent of your income, but some financial advisors will state that 10 percent is fine.

You can divide this up between your retirement plan and between personal savings. What you do with the savings is your personal choice. You can save up to have a nest egg in case something goes wrong, or you can choose to save it for something that you want, for a vacation, or for something else that you need to live your best life.

When you start out on our savings, make sure that you have a clear idea of how you want to work with that savings. Having an end goal in mind can help you to feel accomplished when you get it. If you are saving for retirement, then take the time to set a goal for how much you want to be able to save by the end of the year. If you have a specific goal in mind for the money, then write it down and work towards it. And even if you have multiple goals that you want to reach, make sure that you only use one savings account so you don't end up with more of a mess over time.

The 50/30/20 method is a great option to go with. It helps you to develop some good budgeting habits that can last you a lifetime. It is easy to adopt because it will divide out your income on proportions that are not strict on the numbers. As long as you have an income, you are able to follow it and if your income grows, the proportion will stay the same just with a bigger number to show off that income.

Even though there are these proportions, they are the framework rather than the rule. You can choose which items you want to add into each one, but it gives you the basis that you need to get your finances in order and helps you to set up good budgeting tips that keep you on track. You can always go through and review your self-imposed proportions if you need it or if anything in your goals or finances change.

The 50/30/20 method is one of the best options to work with. It is simple to use and can really keep you on the right budgeting track so you know how to spend your money. If this is the first time that you have ever created a budget, or if you need to find a new method that is going to work well for you, then this may be the method that you need to work with.

Chapter 8:
The Envelope System

W hether you want to use just the cash-only system or you are looking to bring in your spending a bit, the envelop system can be a great minimalist budgeting tool. All that you need for this system is a few envelops, a pen or a pencil, and a copy of the budget that you already set up.

One reason that many people like the envelop system and find it to be effective is that it forces you to use the cash that is on hand to pay for everything. You can't use a credit card here so it really forces you to think about your purchases and whether they are something that will make you happy or not. The point of this method is that your expenses must be limited to the money that you actually have available, either in your bank account or on hand, or you can't purchase the item. When you know that you have limits on how much you can spend rather than putting things on the limitless credit card, you are going to make different decisions with your budget.

The steps to the envelop system

There are a few steps that you can take to get started with the envelop system including:

- Review the budget you want to use: To make this system work, the first thing is to know your budget and the amount that is coming in and out of your home. Start by making sure that your budget is true to your current situation financially. If you haven't taken the time to create a budget, then now is the best time.

- Separate out your expenses: There are some expenses like insurance, rent or mortgage, and utilities that are hard to pay cash for, but the amount will stay the same each month. These should not be part of the envelop system at this time. You can subtract these expenses from your monthly income and pay them separately. The remaining cash that you have needs to get divided between your envelops.

- Decide on the categories: Look over the budget that you have and determine your areas of spending that you are able to cover using cash. This can be entertainment, clothing, gasoline, and food. You can even have a savings envelop if you would like. Make the system work for you. Then have an envelope for each category. A white envelope with the category on the front will be plenty to make this work.

- Fill the envelops: Looking at that budget, fill up each of these envelops with the amount of money that you have allotted for that category. This is all the money that you get to use on that category for the whole month so use it wisely.

- Spend that money in the envelop until it is gone, or until the new month starts: Pay for the purchase out of the right envelop, but only spend until that money is gone. Once you use up the money, no matter what time of the month it is, you can't spend any more in that category until the next month. Since you are actually putting a limit on how much you are allowed to spend in each category, you are going to slow down the purchases you make and only use the money if it is really important to you.

- Put the leftover money into your savings account: If you have a category that has money leftover when the month is done, then add that to your savings account, or use it to pay extra off on a debt. You can also choose to create an additional envelop that is just for your savings. When you review your budget, you can determine how much of it you would like to reserve for your savings envelop.

- Refill at the next month: Once the new month starts, you can refill the envelops and start again. Remember that each month is going to be a new opportunity to make your budget work so even if it didn't work out quite how you planned in the first month, keep trying again.

Following up on your envelop budget

When you first get started on the envelop system, there are going to be some snags that you hit, or there may be a few unexpected expenses that will pop up and make it hard to stick with your plans. Do not worry or panic during this time. Remember that those first few months are going to be tough as you adjust to the changes.

You may learn more about your actual spending

habits, find that you need to reign them in a big more in one area over another, or you may need more money naturally in one area. For example, you may find that in order to feed your family well, you need to put a bit more money in the food category, but a little bit less in the clothing or entertainment budget.

Take the first few months on this type of budgeting system to pay attention to your spending habits and learn how you normally spend money and how much you actually need for your expenses. You can then tweak your allocations to each category during the first few months until you arrive at the numbers that make the most sense for you

If you get started on this process and you are not used to having the cash for all of your purchases, it could take you a bit longer to adjust to this system. Many people are used to working with a credit card, that has an unlimited amount of money that you can use. Cash puts a limit on your spending, which can help you to keep on a budget a little easier but can be hard when you aren't used to the process.

The envelop method can be very effective once you get used to working with it. It just may take you a few months to adjust to this new system. If you have trouble the first few months as you adjust to the system and you run out of money in a category before that month is over, just restart the next month with a fresh budget. You can even make changes to a weekly or bi-weekly envelop system that is based on how often you get a paycheck each month. You get to have some flexibility to the system to go ahead and make some modifications that work well for you.

Chapter 9:
The Snowball Budget Plan

Another method of budgeting that works really well for many people when it comes to paying off debts and helping you to get a bunch of small wins right away in your life is the snowball budget plan. The debt snowball method is a great debt reduction strategy where you are going to pay off your debts going from smallest to largest. This can help you gain some momentum as each balance is paid off. When the smallest debt is paid in full, you will take the money from the payment of that debt and use it towards the next smallest balance. Some of the steps that you will use for the snowball budget plan include:

- List out all of your debts from smallest to largest.

- Make the minimal payments all of your debts, except for the smallest.

- Pay off as much as you can each month on that smallest debt.

- Repeat until each debt is paid in full.

You keep doing this with each debt. If you pay off one of the debts, you then move that money over to the next debt. The process gets faster because you are able to throw more and more money at each debt as you go, and it gives you a lot of motivation because you pay off the smaller debts faster.

An example of using the debt snowball method

To get started and better understand the snowball budget plan, let's take a look at an example of how this budgeting plan can work. Let's say that you have four debts that include the following:

1. A $500 bill for medical visits and you owe $50 a month.

2. $2,500 in debt on your credit cards and you owe $63 a month.

3. $7000 car loan with a payment of $135 a month.

4. $10,000 in student loans and you pay $96 a month.

When you use the debt snowball method, you would make the minimum payments on everything except for your medical bill. Let's say that you took on a side job or that you made enough and cut down your expenses so you were able to pay an extra $500 a month on the debts.

In this example, you are able to pay $550 on the medical bill and that one will be done within one month. You then take that $550 and start putting it towards the credit card. You would add this $550 to the $63 minimum payment that you are already doing, resulting in a payment that is $613 a month. In about four months, the credit card payment is going to be completely paid off.

Now that those first two debts are paid off, you can start putting about $748 towards that car loan (the $613 from the previous loans and then the $135 added to it). This will then take you ten months to pay off the car loan and own the car outright.

By the time that you get to your biggest loan in this situation, the student loan, you are able to put $844 a month towards it, and you are still just paying the amount that you did in the beginning when you started with the medical bill. This amount can help you pay off the remainder of your student loan debts in just 12 months.

In this example, you are able to pay off $20,000 in debt fairly quickly. You get it done in just 27 months using the snowball method and then can live a life free of debt. And if you are able to put more money aside each month towards the debts, you could get them paid off even faster! You could keep using that side job or cutting expenses and put all that money towards savings and other things that you want to do, or you can choose to cut out that side job and just enjoy some of the extra freedom that you gain with no debt.

Why does this method work so well?

This method works because it is more about modifying your behavior and not all about the math. With the example above, if you had started paying off the largest debt, the student loan, you wouldn't see the debt disappear for a bit. The numbers are going down, but you aren't able to make as large of payments on it and you will lose steam and stop paying extra on those debts. It may help limit your overall payment in interest, but it is more about helping you see progress quickly.

When you pay off the smaller debts first, you are going to see a lot more progress. You have one debt that is out of your life for good. Then you can keep up the momentum and other debts will follow. As you see that the method is working, you are more likely to stick with it. By the time that you get to those larger debts, there is a ton more cash available from those earlier debts that you paid off that you create a debt snowball. This builds up momentum and this can really work to change your behavior and makes it easier to get rid of that debt in your life once and for all.

You can choose how much extra you are able to pay off. The example that we did is talking about $500, but you can pay more or less. Even a few extra dollars a month, or whatever you can afford, will be enough to make this method work. Just remember that the more you are able to pay towards you're your debts, the faster they will be gone. Consider a side job, find places you can cut things out in your budget, and do what you can to finally get rid of those debts so that you can really enjoy your life and not be burdened by all those extra debts that are hanging around.

The snowball debt management method is a great one to work with. It allows you the freedom to pay off debts and see a lot of success quickly, and it can give you the momentum that you need to pay off everything. You don't have to worry so much about the math and which debts should be done first, it is more about working in a way that changes your behaviors and gives you a reward for your hard work.

Chapter 10:
Reverse Budgeting

G etting started on a budget and sticking with it can be really hard because it takes a lot of time and puts restrictions on them. It would be nice to just spend the amount that we want and not worry about a budget at all. But for most people, there is a limit on how much you have available to spend, which means that a budget is a necessity. Traditional budgeting forces you to make your spending decisions like you live on a spreadsheet, but since most people don't live their lives this way, it is sometimes better to find a different method.

Rather than focusing on all your expenses, it is better for many people to focus on their savings. This can be done through a process known as reverse budgeting. This type of budgeting allows you to figure out how much you need to save, and then you will automate those savings. The remaining amount of money in your account can be spent the way that you want.

With this method, if you spent the budgeted amount on eating out and entertainment, but then there was something important but unexpected that comes up and you need to dine out, this method allows you to shift your spending from somewhere else to help you still stay in line with your current values and priorities.

Because this type of budgeting is going to focus on saving, you get into a situation where you aren't able to spend what you don't have. Increasing how much you save is going to naturally reduce the amount that you are able to spend and it is going to force you to prioritize the things you spend your money on. This is important because a gradual increase in savings makes it possible for them to cut out some spending that doesn't really fit with their values, without feeling overwhelmed in the beginning.

The best thing with reverse budgeting is that it won't require you to keep up with a lot of maintenance t make it work. A traditional budget requires you to have a weekly or a monthly reconciliation of all your finances. But once you get the reverse budget set up, you can automate everything. The time commitment is much less, which is what helps you to stick with this reverse budget better than before.

If you are interested in implementing a reverse budget in your life, there are a few steps that you can take. These include:

Add up the amount that you need to save every month to reach your goals

The first step is to write down a goal and the estimated date that you want to reach it. Having the cost associated with it can really help as well. It can also help you to get a better understanding of the items that you hold the most important to yourself.

You can start with some short-term goals, ones that need to take place in the next five years or less. Then write down the desired date of completion and the amount that it will cost you. If you add up all your expected costs to reach your goals, you can then figure out how much you will need to save each month to make these goals a reality. You can pick any goal that you would like but use this to help you figure out how much you need to put into savings each month to reach these goals.

You can also do this exercise with things like intermediate goals, ones that you want to complete between five to fifteen years, and then long-term goals. You can also choose to redo the budget every year or so to encompass some modern goals that come up and to make changes as you pay things down. If you don't make enough to meet your monthly savings requirement for the short-term goals, you may try to slowly escalate your savings over time. You can also make some adjustments to your goals to help make them more realistic.

Set up automated withdrawals to the savings account.

Next, you can open up a savings account (an online one can work really well). Try to find one that pays a higher interest rate as well. Set up an automatic monthly withdrawal from your checking account over to that new savings account each month. Set it up to withdraw the amount that you wish to save back based on the first step. Then, whatever money is left in the checking account, can be used in any way that you want.

Escalate the automatic savings over time

This can be a powerful tool for those who want to really add some power to their savings plans and those who aren't able to set aside the full amount that they want to meet those short-term goals. Escalating your savings is a good way to slowly advance yourself towards the ideal monthly savings. Start by setting up a few automatic withdrawals from the checking account into the savings account. You would start the first three months with $100 each month. Then your second set would withdraw $150 a month. And then $200 a month and so on over the next year.

If you were able to start the reverse budget saving your ideal monthly amount, you could still escalate it over time to help you get some of those intermediate and long term goals that you have. And it never hurts to save back more and help yourself really limit the amount you spend on the things that you really need, rather than falling pretty to a bunch of unnecessary purchases.

The reverse budgeting method is a great option to help promote savings, helps you to reach some of your financial goals, and it doesn't require as much planning and time commitment as some of the other methods. You simply need to pick out the financial goals that you want to meet, as well as a date for them, and put that money into savings. Then use the leftover money to deal with everything else that needs taken care of during the month.

Chapter 11:
The 80/20 Budget

I f you like the ideas that come with the 50/30/20 budget, but you feel that you need something else to help you, then there is a close alternative that is known as the 80/20 budget. With this budget plan, you are going to take 20 percent of your income, no matter how much you make, towards savings. The other 80 percent of your budget needs to be used to pay for everything else such as your bills and extra spending.

One nice thing about this plan, like with the other option, is that you don't have to spend as much time tracking your expenses. You just need to see how much you made for the month (or bi-weekly) and then put 20 percent of that towards your savings account before you pay any of your bills or do anything else with the money.

How this plan is going to work in real life

The next question is how this type of budget play will work in real life. The easiest way to make this happen is to set up an automatic withdrawal so that the 20 percent leaves your checking account and moves the money to your savings account. You want to have this withdrawal happen a few days after each payday to help you get started.

Now, if you don't have a regular paycheck or the amount changes each pay period, then take a look at how much you brought in at the beginning of the month, or whenever you get paid. Then take twenty percent of that amount and move it right over to your savings before you do anything else. After the money is moved over to savings, you can use the rest of it in any way that you would like. You can pay your bills, go get some fun things, go out to eat, or whatever you need to with the money that is left while knowing you still get to keep that nice amount in savings.

The biggest problem is if you have a savings account that is already linked to your checking account. This makes it easy to move that money right aver to the checking account when you overspend and can eat into the money you should be saving. You may want to consider transferring the money to a different bank. This way you won't automatically see the amount in the account when you open the page, and it takes a few days before you can use that money.

You also don't need to put all of your savings into a traditional savings account. You could put it towards your retirement account to give you a head start. You can also redirect the money into a brokerage account and earn some extra interest on the money that you aren't using right that moment.

Many people who decide to go on the 80/20 budget will put a lot of their savings towards a retirement. The earlier you can start with the retirement plan, the more financially secure you will be in your later years. You can choose the amount that you would like to move into a retirement plan. If you have some other big financial goals, such as purchasing a home, then maybe consider splitting up the savings 50/50 so half goes to this goal and half goes to the retirement plan that you want to use. Even this amount, the ten percent, towards your retirement in your 20's can really help you to get a lot of money saved up by the time you reach your 60s.

You can choose how you would like to deal with your savings. If you have a lot of debts that you want to pay down or a few financial goals that you want to hit first, then you may want to only put a few percentage points of your income towards your retirement and the rest towards your financial goals. Or you can choose to split these percentages out a bit differently. Consider putting aside 25 or 30 percent of your income towards savings and then only using the rest of that towards your bills and other spending.

The reason that this plan works so well is that it is so simple. You only have to keep track of two numbers and you are automatically putting some money into savings when you do it. With the eighty percent, you can pay off your bills and then use the rest of the money in any way that you want. You don't have to spend a lot of time worrying about every penny you spend. You don't have to split it up into different categories at all. You just have to remember that the money that is in the account is all that you get until the next month.

Take it even further

The 80/20 rule is a good place to start. It automatically helps you to have some money in savings, without having to think about it too much. You can add it just to one account or start saving for your retirement if you choose. There are no wrong answers for what you can do with the savings, just keep it separate from your bill and fun money.

But you may want to consider taking it even further. This can be helpful if you really want to cut out the extra and unnecessary spending that you do each month or if you have some large financial goals that you want to reach quickly. Adding in some more money to your savings can be just the trick that you need to handle these situations.

For example, once you have had some time to achieve the 80/20 method and it has been pretty successful for you, then you can put yourself to a 70/30 savings rate or a 60/40 savings rate. You can push this as much as you want and the more that you pay off your debts, the more you can put into your savings at the end of the month.

Remember with this method that the more you put into savings, the more flexibility and opportunity you will have to do the things that you really want to do. You can make your retirement bigger, you can retire earlier, you could purchase rental properties, start your own business, or even go on a vacation. The more that you can push yourself and add money to savings, the easier it will be to have the financial life that you want.

Chapter 12:
The Zero-Based Budgeting

Another type of budget that you can choose to work with is known as a zero-based budget. This is when you take your income and minus out all your expenses to equal zero. You want to make sure that your expenses match what income you will bring in each month and that every dollar has some kind of function. This doesn't mean that you need to keep zero dollars in the bank account. But it should mean that your income minus all your expenses at the end of the month should be zero.

This means that if you bring in $3000 a month, you want to take everything and either spend it, save it, give it, or invest it until you have used all $3000. This helps you to keep track of every dollar that you earn. This may take a bit more work compared to some of the other methods, but for some people who need to have full control over their money, it is the best option. It ensures that you never go through your bank account and wonder where all the money has gone.

How to work on your zero-based budget

There are a few steps that you can follow when you are ready to start making a zero-based budget for your needs. Some of the steps that you can follow with this method include:

Write down your monthly income

You can do this the traditional method and use a sheet of paper, or you can find a good budgeting app online that will help you out. You need to first collect all your income, including any cash you bring in like paychecks, income from a small-business or a side hustle, residual income, and child support. If it is money and it comes into your bank account, you need to count this as income. Write it down and then add it up in your budget.

Write down what you must spend your money on each month

Now that you know what your monthly income is, it is time to keep track of your expenses. Before the new month begins, write down all of the expenses that you have. This would include some of the necessary expenses, like rent, cable, phones, and food. Your budget is going to look a bit different than everyone else's based on the bills and debts you have, but make sure that it starts with what is known as the Four Walls – food, transportation, basic clothing, and shelter and utilities. Everyone has to pay these in their budget to make sure they get written down in the budget first.

After those essentials are covered, it is time to list out the rest of your expenses each month. The needs that you encounter every month can change, which is why you should create a new spending plan each month. This can help keep you from feeling overwhelmed because you only need to focus on one month at a time.

Write down the seasonal expenses

Now you can take a look at the whole year and determine which expenses may be coming up that you might want to plan for now. You know that Christmas is in December and that birthdays occur at the same time every year. There is no reason to get all worried about them sneaking up on you because it is easy to plan them out. No matter what occasion you are working on, make sure that you prepare for those expenses in your budget. Just make sure that you schedule them in and plan ahead so you can afford them.

Next, there are also going to be some irregular expenses that may pop up in your budget. You can plan for these as well. Things like property taxes, car tag renewal fees, and insurance premiums are things that you can budget for. If you set aside a little bit for this every month, you won't feel the strain as much when these expenses do come due.

Take your income and subtract it from the expenses to get zero

When you take your income from all your expenses, you want the number to end up being zero. It can take a bit of practice before you reach this. You don't need to be worried if these don't end up balancing each other out right away. This just means that you need to bring one of these sides up, the other one down, or a combination of both. This takes some work, but getting it written down can really help.

First, if you see that you spend more than you make, it is time to trim up the budget to get the income and the outgoing money get to zero. To help you cut back on your expenses, find what you can live without, use coupons, cut the cable, purchase generic products at the store, carpool to work and so on. If you have trimmed the spending as much as possible, then consider selling stuff around the house (if you are doing minimalism you are getting rid of a lot of clutter anyway) or find a side job to get yourself organized.

This is the thing about zero-based budgeting though. Each dollar that you earn must go somewhere. You should not finish this and be positive or negative at all. You can add more to your savings or more to giving if you want, but make sure that all of the money you earn is going somewhere and that you know where that area is.

Track your spending and get started

All that you need to do now is make sure that you track the expenses that you have through the month. This is the best and only way that you will know if your spending is lining up with your plan. This is how you will start winning with money throughout not just the month, but also throughout the whole year. When you track your expenses and engage with your money, it is easier to make progress with your budgeting and learn how to love your life. And you will no longer be scared each time you check out your bank account.

Is it possible to use this method when your income is irregular?

Some people have an income that is pretty much the same every month, but others who freelance or get paid hourly may find that they don't always make the same amount every month. The good news is that you can still use this method even if your income isn't regular. The best way to do this is to figure out what a low earning month is like and then create the budget based on this month, even if you do have better months as well.

You still need to make sure that you cover the four walls, just like we talked about above, and then list out the rest of the expenses based on how important they are. Then, when you do get paid, you can take that amount and spread it out over all the items. Sometimes, your paycheck isn't going to cover all the items you listed in your budget, but that isn't a big deal. You just need to cover the items that are the most important, such as your housing payment.

With an irregular income, there will be times when you make more and times when you make less. On those lower months, you must make sure that you cover at least the major expenses and bills. But on the good months, you can cover all the expenses and then add more towards your debts and to saving more to help cover those slow months.

Why is this method so important?

Having a budget, or your own detailed spending plan is one of the best and quickest ways to help reach all your financial goals. If you want to get out of debt, you need a budget. If you want to put some money into savings, then you need a budget. If you want to purchase a home, plan for retirement, or do anything with your finances, then you need to set up a budget.

You are the boss of your budget, but if you just throw money in the account and then never assign it to where you want it to go, your money will seem to disappear. You need to be there to tell every dollar where you want it to go. This isn't meant to limit the freedom that you have. Instead, you gain more freedom because you know where the money goes and can get it to stretch out further than before.

The zero-based budget is a great one to go with, especially for those who often check their bank account and then wonder where all their money goes. You are the boss of your money and it can only be spent when you want it and where you want it to. This method of budgeting ensures that every dollar is accounted ahead of time. This way, you can stretch your budget as far as possible and you never have to be worried where the money went.

Chapter 13:
The Cash-Only Budget

M ost traditional budgets are going to require a lot of discipline. If you have found that you overspend in many of the categories of your budget, this may be a sign that the budget choice you made isn't working. A cash only budget can be a good option because it is a low-maintenance way to ensure that you will reach your financial goals. You have to stop using your credit cards, debit cards, and every other form of payment and just rely on the cash that you have from your income to make the purchases you need. Let's take some time to look at the cash only system and how it can work for you.

How the cash only budget works

A cash only budget means that you will only use cash for all your spending needs. You are not allowed to use debit cards, credit cards, or even checks to make your purchase. This is often paired along with the envelop budgeting system that we talked about before. But you can also change it up. With the envelop system you will separate your budget into categories and then can only spend that much in the categories. But with cash only budgeting, you could just lump all your available money in one and then that has to last for everything you need for the month.

Before you get started with the cash-only budget, it is a good idea to put a basic budget in place. This is important to ensure you withdraw the right amount of cash each month. If you take out too much, you may not have enough for savings or for any bills you have to pay online. Once you know your budget, you can withdraw the leftover money and use that for your monthly needs.

Using this method can help with your spending

The biggest benefit that you will get with this method of budgeting is that it can help you to stick to the budget better. Since you can actually see how much money is left throughout the month. When you notice the money is running out, you are more likely to be frugal and try to hold onto it more. The money is right there, rather than hidden in the bank, so it is harder to ignore.

There is something powerful in the minds of most people about handling over cash compared to swiping a card, and even research can prove this. Think about it, do you enjoy seeing the number of bills you have shrink? Probably not. For most people, it is painful to hand over cash to someone else rather than swipe your card.

The psychology that comes with this method of budgeting is something that you shouldn't ignore. It is more impactful compared to checking your spending with the help of a budgeting software or tracking it on a spreadsheet. Both of these are going to happen after the fact. You will make the purchase and then go through writing down the amount later on. You may feel guilty or remorse when you write it down, but since it happens after the fact, we can't do anything to change it. When you use cash, you can feel the guilt right then and there and you will do everything you can to avoid that if possible.

Can help you pay off debt faster

A cash only budget can be a great option for those dealing with credit card debt. If you have issues with swiping your card too often, then it may be a better option to stick with cash. This can help you start out some good spending habits. Plus, you can use those good spending habits to make it easier to pay off those credit card debts, and other debts, faster. Getting a good handle on your spending could help you find some extra money in your budget, money that you can use to pay off debt faster.

You must think about your purchases ahead of time.

A cash only budget can also help those who are impulse shoppers. When you are limited in the amount of money that you can use for the whole month, you will need to focus more on your purchases and think them through. You aren't allowed to dip into the credit card or your savings with this method, so when it comes to deciding between that impulse buy and food for the month, you may think twice about getting an item you don't need.

This barrier that deters spending can be a great way to get your spending in check and can make it easier for you to live a minimalistic lifestyle. You will be less likely to purchase items that you don't need, items that are just going to create a lot of clutter around the home. You will save your money for things that you actually value, things that make your life happier, rather than purchasing things that you don't need.

After you use a cash only budget for just a few months, it won't be hard to recognize the weak points where you have some concerns about your spending. For example, you may find that you have trouble sticking to your clothes budget, but your gas budget is easy. Or you spend too much at fast food stops because you like to eat out.

With your normal spending patterns, you may not think twice about these budget leaks. But with the idea of a cash only budget, you need to think more about what you spend your money on and where and whether you need to readjust some of your goals or if you just need to readjust the way that you spend money. For example, if you enjoy eating out with friends and family, do you need to allocate some more money to this each month to fulfil your life, or would you do just as well with making more meals at home and saving that money? Each person will do this differently, you just need to decide what works for you.

The cash only system can work well because it forces you to physically hand over the money that you earn each month, rather than having it just disappear off a card. This can put you more in control of the money that you have and can make it harder for you to give into impulse buys. Consider implementing this along with your chosen budget so you can really reign in your spending and see good results.

Chapter 14:
Goals That Can Help You Set a SMART Budget

SMART goals

Now it is time to think about some of your goals. One of the first steps that come with creating the best budget is to know your goals ahead of time. These goals need to be money related at this point. It is fine to make goals for other parts of your life, but for now, we just want to take a look at your financial goals. Do you want to save enough money for a house, for a car, or just to have an emergency fund? Do you want to pay off any debts? Do you want to put some money back to help pay for college?

As you work on your budget, you will find that it is not always easy. It involves a lot of difficult choices, painful compromises, and more. Still, having a goal before you get started can help you see the promise that all the sacrifices you make are worth it, and this helps make the process of budgeting seem less painful.

One of the best ways for you to set your financial goals is to follow what is known as the SMART goal technique. The SMART acronym stands for Specific, Measurable, Achievable, Relevant, and Time. Financial goals, just like other goals, can be divided up into short term, long term, and even intermediate term if you would like. You can set these up for your needs to ensure that you are dealing with your finances the right way and reaching all the financial goals that you have.

Any goal that you decide to work on needs to be a SMART goal. This ensures that it is one that is actually something that you can work on. You shouldn't pick out a goal that says you want to put money in savings at some time. Instead, say how much you want to save, when you want to do it by, and what you will use that money for. This gives you something to work towards.

Where is the money coming from

Discovering the SMART goal is just the first step here. You then need to dig a bit deeper and learn your current financial reality. To do this, you can collect all your income sources and then make a list of them including work, loans, parents, interest payments, royalties and so on. You can't make some smart goals if you have no idea where your money is coming from.

When you look through your income, you need to figure out if this is pretty standard or if the income is variable. If your income is pretty regular, you will be able to use this information and keep it pretty similar for each month that you budget. But if your income is variable, you may need to work on the budget a bit differently each month to deal with the changes that occur in your income from one month to the next.

Where is the money going?

After you have taken time to figure out all your income sources and where your money is coming from, you can then take a look at where the money is going. You can categorize your expenses in the manner that works the best for you. But write them all down. You need to write out everything that you spend your money each month.

You can group them all together in one category, or you can separate them out. Some people like to group together all their necessities, such as the mortgage, utilities, phone, food, and debts in one category. These are the bills that they have to pay each month and are the ones they most budget for. These bills often don't change much, if at all, from one month to another. No matter which budgeting method you choose to go with, these are the expenses that need to be taken care of first.

Next on the list is the other expenses that you may have. This could include your savings, clothing, birthdays and holidays, gas, entertainment, and paying extra on debts. These have a bit of variability in them and some, such as the entertainment, can be lightened a bit if you have a leaner month. No matter which method you go with, make sure that you list out all of the expenses that you can think of for the month and then list based on how important they are.

Be flexible

It is important to come up with a good budget to follow, if you notice that one plan isn't working well for you or if there is a better way to do it, then it is fine to change it up. There needs to be some flexibility in your budgeting plan. This isn't an excuse to just throw it out the window and use your income however you want. But if you find the budgeting plan too strict or you find somewhere else that would be pretty easy to cut from, then go ahead and do this.

You also need to take your personal income into account. You have to pay your mortgage and your utilities and other bills. If these amounts take up a lot of your income, you may not be able to put the 20 to 30 percent back for savings like some of the plans require. Putting anything back is a great way to prepare you for the future though, so even if it is just a few dollars a month, you are going to get ahead. But if your income doesn't allow you to follow a particular budget plan, then it is fine to adjust and make it work for you.

A SMART budget is going to include some goals that help you get to the financial future that you want. Many of these are easy to understand, but if your income or your situation doesn't allow you to reach them right in the beginning, maybe consider putting that down as your goal. Before you get started on a new budget plan or following any of the advice that we provide in this guidebook, sit down and determine your short-term, medium-term, and long-term goals and then work from there to help you refocus your budget to fit your needs.

Chapter 15:
How to Maintain Your
Minimalist Budget

U sing some of the methods that we have talked about in this guidebook, you should have a great budget in mind. You should know how you are going to spend your money and how much you will have available for your debts, your bills, your savings, and more. That can take some time to accomplish and you need to give yourself some time to get used to these changes. But after you get through the beginning excitement of creating the budget, it is important for you to be able to maintain all your plans. A budget won't do you much good if you can't stick with it beyond a few months. Let's take a look at some of the steps that you can take to help you not only create your minimalist budget, but also stick with it for the long-term.

How to maintain your budget

The first thing that you may want to consider is to carry the budget around with you. Unless you have a good memory, you will need to carry around the budget, whether that is in a hard copy or in an electronic form. Or at least bring a few of your envelops with you as a reminder if you use this method. Then, when you are out shopping and that new dress or pair of shoes calls your name, you can pull out your budget and see if that item is actually worth it?

If the dress is going to cost you $200, you can look at the budget and see that to do this, you have to sacrifice date night or your monthly visit to the salon. Taking the time to analyze your budget and determine whether the item is worth it, you may find that the item looks less appealing than before.

Another option is to carry around a calculator with you. Daily errands, such as going to the grocery store, can really cause trouble with your budget if you are not careful. Take that calculator along with you when working on things like grocery shopping. You can keep a running total of how much the items in your cart cost as you move through the store.

If you use this method and find that you are through your weekly budget and you still haven't made it through the store, then you may need to reconsider some of your purchases. When this happens, it's most likely because you have added too many items that you don't need and it may be time to add a few more back to the shelf. Look to see if you grabbed too many sales items that you didn't need if you grabbed too many snacks, and whether you could switch some of your options out for something that costs less. Make it your goal to stick at or under your weekly budget while at the store.

In the beginning, it is a good idea to read through your budget on a weekly basis. This means that you should pick a time once a week when you can sit down and review your budget and determine if it is still realistic or not. If you find that after a month or two you seem to exceed your limits in a category, then it may be time to readjust the amount that you allow yourself in this category or take a look at ways that you can cut in that area. But remember that doing this will mean that you need to sacrifice in some of your other categories.

What this means is if your dry cleaning bill may be $20 a week, but you only budgeted out $10, and you are not able to go through and reduce this fee, then you may need to reduce how much you are allowed to spend on entertainment or even on new clothes. If you don't want to do this, it may be time to consider only doing dry cleaning every other week or cutting out dry cleaning for your clothes all together.

There are always going to be some special events that come up in your budget. And most of them, such as birthdays and holidays, are things that you are going to know about ahead of time. If you know that a holiday is coming up, or that you have a wedding in a few months, you can plan ahead. If you plan to get a new outfit for that occasion, find ways to cut $10 out of your clothing budget each week leading up to the wedding. This only takes a little bit that you will barely notice, and you will have the money that you need for a new outfit.

As you are working on your budget, make sure that you put a little bit back to help out if you have any expenses that you weren't prepared for. It is often recommended that you save a minimum of $1000 in your emergency fund. There are a lot of different expenses that can come up, and you need to pay for them. But when they are unexpected, they can mess with even the best thought out budgets.

If you have an emergency fund set up, you can handle those expenses. You may have a minor medical emergency come up, a funeral you need to travel to another state for, or something goes wrong with your vehicle. You can use that emergency fund to help you to pay for these expenses and help you to not have to stress out as much as possible.

One of the best ways to help you manage and maintain your budget is to go through and review it on a regular basis. You do not want to rely on the same budget for years on end. Sometimes the plan that you choose is not going to fit your needs. Sometimes it may be too hard to maintain for you and you need to go with a different method. Or you may even pay off some debts or make more income. All of these changes can affect the budgeting method that you choose and checking up on it can be a great option.

You have to choose how often you want to review your budget. When you first get started, it may be a good idea to review the budget every month. This gives you some insight into your spending habits and can help you to make changes to your budget pretty quickly. But after you have had some time to adjust to the budget and you have a plan that you like, consider looking through the budget every six months or so.

This review can be helpful. If you make more money since you last looked at your budget, determine where to add the new money or if you just want to keep the categories the same and add the money to your savings. If you pay off a few debts, it may be time to readjust the financial goals that you have. Even if you don't end up making any changes to your budget, it can still be helpful to take a look at it and check where you are and how far you have come.

Some more tips to help you maintain your budget

It isn't enough to just go through and create a budget and try it for one or two months. You also need to maintain your budget for the long term. You need to really work on this and keep it going if you really want to get the most out of it. Over time, a good budget can help you to save money, pay down debts, and stop all those unnecessary purchases. Some of the other steps that you can take to help you maintain your budget and get the most out of your hard work includes the following:

- Continue to find ways to save money and cut expenses from your budget: There are a lot of different things that you are able to cut from your budget, but the one that you choose is going to vary based on your usual circumstances. Pick out the ones that you are most comfortable with dropping and see what a difference it can be.

- Try to avoid splurges Avoid things that are on sale. Only purchase what you really need or what will really bring you happiness. Anything else will just waste money and require you to keep it up and clean it all the time.

- If you do happen to go over on your budget one month, then learn from it. Try to figure out why you went over budget and what you can do in the following month to avoid this happening again.

- Consider how much you would want to put back into savings: It is always a good idea to put some of your income into savings. This can help you prepare in case there is some kind of emergency, can help you pay off debts a bit faster, and can provide you with peace of mind. Some experts recommend ten percent, some recommend twenty percent and some would want higher amounts. The important part is that something goes into savings so make it work for your income.

- Start putting aside money to help with a larger purchase or a vacation: This should be put away separate from your regular savings. This will make sure that you don't end up depleting your savings.

- Do an occasional evaluation of your income again. You don't want to set up a budget and then leave it the same for the next ten to twenty years. Your finances are going to change during that time. You may make more money, you may pay off some debts, and the price of your regular expenses will change. Once or twice a year, go over your budget and determine if there is anything that needs to be changed to help you stay on track.

While creating a budget is a good first step, you also need to take things a bit further to ensure that once that budget is in place, you can also keep with it and not fall into your old habits again. Use the tips in this chapter to help you to keep that budget in line to see the best results!

Chapter 16:
The 60% Budget

T his method is similar to the balanced money formula or the 50/30/20 budget because it will help you to use percentages to manage your current finances rather than relying on a specific dollar amount. Using these percentages makes it easier for you to include these methods no matter how much income you are able to bring in. The 60 percent solution is a bit different than the other methods, but it can help you to change up the way that you budget and separate out the expenses that you need to take care of.

How this method works

To start, the sixty percent that is talked about in the name is going to be used for your committed expenses. These are going to include some expenses like insurance, car payments, basic clothing, food, and your mortgage. Where this is going to be different from the needs category in the 50/30/20 method is that this sixty percent is going to include all of your bills. Everything that you need to pay each month will be included in the sixty percent. This would include things like debt as well so make sure that you include this in there.

The rest of your income, or the other forty percent, needs to be divided up into four other categories. You should allocate ten percent to each category, but if it works better for your long term financial goals to change up the percentage than go ahead and do this. The four categories that you should use for this part include:

- Retirement: You should save at least ten percent of your income for a retirement plan. You can choose the retirement plan that works best for you, but a 401K and a Roth IRA are the two most popular options. If you have the option, get this amount taken out of your paycheck each pay period so you don't have to think about doing the work yourself.

- Long-term savings: This would include things like your emergency fund, saving money for your down payment on a home, and other things that may take you more than five years to accomplish. if you have some larger debts that you want to pay off faster, then you can add some of the money in your savings to help with this goal as well.

- Short-term savings: You can also consider having a short-term savings account to help you reach some of your goals. This is a separate account that you can easily access if you need to transfer funds back to your checking account. This would include options like bigger expenses that pop up, irregular expenses, and even vacations. The idea with this savings is that you would use up all the money within a year.

- Fun money: This is the last part of your forty percent. This is where some of your entertainment, dining, and extras are going to come in. these are expenses that you could cut back on if your income is smaller one month and they are things that you don't have to pay. Sure, it is fine to go out to eat, but you can certainly survive without doing it if needed.

For the most part, it is best if you can keep the percentages pretty even here. Don't try to add more money to the fun money area because then you may start to give in to unnecessary purchases. If your income increases, than just increase all the category amounts as well. If you can, cut down your commitment expenses a bit and divide that money between your savings accounts so you can reach your short term and your long term goals faster than before.

Who would benefit from this budget?

This budget plan does work well for a lot of people. If you like the idea of automating a lot of your bills, then this works well. You can automatically have money taken out of your account for retirement, for bills, and for your two savings account. Then the only thing that you need to deal with is how to spend that last ten percent to help you with your fun money.

In addition, you are only allowed to use about sixty percent of your income for your bills. This is often enough money to handle your bills if you work on it, but it also leaves enough so that you can save a ton more money than usual. It is similar to giving yourself an artificial pay cut and then spending your time living paycheck to paycheck since you cut down your income so much.

Since you are going to concentrate more on percentages with this method, there could be some temptation that is built in to not track your expenses. You have your bills taken care of, which will be the first sixty percent, and then your savings (split up between retirement, long term savings, and short term savings) and then your fun money isn't allowed to go over ten percent.

This does allow for a lot of automation and can

make things easier to handle. But it also allows you to just ignore your money and not pay attention to it. No matter which method you choose to go with, it is important to still track your expenses to make sure that you never go above the amount of money that you originally budgeted.

At the very least, take the time to watch that ten percent that is used for fun money. Since so much of your budget is automated with this option, it may be easy to go over on the ten percent, which could ruin your budget overall. Make sure that you really watch the fun money to keep you on track. You can consider using the cash only method just for your fun money so you know when the money is used up and you have to stop.

Overall, for those who want to make things a little more automated and who don't want to get into the most complicated parts of budgeting, this sixty percent method may be the right one for you. It ensures that all your basis are covered, allows you to save more money than ever before, and just makes life easier in the process. It is definitely one of the methods that you should consider if you are still looking for the right budgeting method for you.

Chapter 17:
The No Budget Method

And now it is time to look at the final budgeting method that we are going to discuss in this guidebook. The only thing that you need to pay attention to with this method is the balance in your bank account. You don't even need to track all the individual expenses. This is a really simple method because it just requires you to watch your balance and learn when the money is getting low. This may not be the best method for everyone, but it can work for some people.

This one is going to slightly overlap with the sixty percent method because you are going to automate your savings and you must check that you have enough in your account at a time to cover all your necessary bills, like food, mortgages, and other debts. But everything else that is left in the account after these things are taken care of can be spent in any way that you want.

To start, you need to go through and look at the income that is in your account. Then you can add up your bills and make sure there is enough in the account to cover them. Automate your savings out of that amount as well. Then subtract these amounts from the total in the bank account. Anything else that is left in the account can be used in any manner that you choose. Simply watch the account because once the money is gone, you can't spend any more.

Who would benefit from this budgeting method?

This is a budgeting method that works well for those who aren't really that in to budgeting. If you don't like to figure out all the numbers or you don't want to put in the time to budget down to every dollar that you earn and how it is spent, then this might be the right method for you. It really doesn't require a lot of work on your part and only a little bit of tracking to make sure you don't overspend with the money that you have.

While most people need to track their spending a bit more and they find that having every dollar accounted for can work out better, this can help save a lot of time. In addition, it often works for those who make a little bit more because they know they will have enough to cover the bills and some of their fun times without having to worry about running out of money.

What should I watch out for?

Since the No Budget method is not having you pay close attention to the expenses that you incur, there is some danger if you like to overspend. It is important that you choose to prioritize your saving if you go on this method. Then you can use those savings to help out if you end up overspending or if there is something unexpected that pops up that you need to handle. Consider putting an emergency fund in place before you decide to go with this method to keep you safe as you adjust to it.

The no budget method is only going to work for some people. Most people need to have a big more accountability to make things work and this method is a bit more laid back. But it can be helpful for those who want to keep things as simple as possible and who don't want to spend all their time worrying about their budge.t if you are good at not overspending and you make enough for this method, it may be worth taking a look at.

Chapter 18:
Tips to Help You Get the Most Out of Any Budgeting Plan You Choose

There are a lot of different budgeting plans that you can choose from. Hopefully, you have found one that is going to provide you with the benefits that you need to see success. But no matter which method you go with, the following tips can ensure that you can maximize the benefits of the method and get the best results from them:

- Know the reasons why you are budgeting: If you are getting started on your budget just because someone suggested it as a good idea, then it probably isn't going to work well for you. Have a good reason why you are budgeting and use this as a motivation to keep yourself on track.

- Have some good long-term goals in mind: Many people set their goal as debt freedom. But you could also choose some options like saving for a house, having the ability to start their own business, or something else. You can choose any goal that you want, but make sure that it is concrete and something that you can actually follow.

- Know the exact amount that you make: You do not want to just assume that you know how much money you make each month. You are probably wrong. Some people overestimate their income, forgetting that they may have a certain amount put back for taxes, social security, and even retirement. Go through and write down the exact amount that you bring home each month, or each paycheck, before you even think about starting on your budget.

- Look at your bank statements: Just like you can't estimate how much income you bring in, you can't assume or estimate the amount that you spend each month. Getting bank statements out can give you the best idea of this. Bring out all your bills, your receipts, and your bank statements for the last six to twelve minutes so that you can see your spending. Then your new budget can include all of these expenses and allows you some options when it comes to cutting things out if you need. When doing this, make sure to count some of your irregular bills, some of the ones that don't show up each month. This could include your car licenses, property taxes, and more. When you figure these into your budget, they won't come as such a surprise when you need to pay for them.

- Consider having savings and checking accounts that include budgeting tools: This can make it easier to stick with your budget and can even show you some charts about how much you have saved, how much you spend and on what, and so much more. Every bank is going to offer some different tools. If your current savings or checking accounts don't offer some of these tools, it may be time to shop around for something better. And while you do this, check and see if you can find an account that offers a higher interest rate than your current bank.

- Pick out a budgeting tool that you

understand how to use: There are so many different options when it comes to picking out the right budgeting tool. You can use an app, a tool online, a simple calculator, or even a pen and paper. All of them can work well. But you need to pick the one that works for you. If you find that simplicity is the best, then pen and paper can do the job. But if you like to have lots of options and everything listed out well, then you may want to find an online app that can help with this option.

- Always keep things realistic: Budgeting can work well for you, but you can run into trouble if you try to make big and unrealistic assumptions in the beginning, or your goals are too hard to reach based on your current income and bills. You are not going to be able to pay off $50,000 extra in debts if you only earn $75,000 and have to spend $55,000 on regular debts and bills. You also won't be able to heavily reduce one category of your spending overnight. Don't assume that you can completely get rid of your entertainment budget if you like to go out with friends all the time. Cutting categories by about five to ten percent is a good place to start and you can always cut them lower later on.

- Find someone who can support you: When you look around you and see that so many people are into materialistic items, it can be really hard to stick with the budget that you want. You will want to go out there and get the latest gadget or item and may feel deprived if you are the only one who doesn't get to do this. But this is not a smart way to live a minimalistic life and can make it hard to stay on the budget that you want.

If you find someone to do the budgeting with you, or at least someone who will support you along the way, you will find that it gets easier. Both of you can support each other, offer advice, and encourage each other to ensure that you stick with your plan.

- Cut up the credit cards: Many Americans rely on credit cards to make their purchases. They may promise to only use it to get their points, but often this fails miserably. Instead, they keep putting more and more purchases on the card, not paying attention to the balance at the end of the month and not even purchasing anything that they really need. Instead of relying on cards, switch to the cash only system and then cut up the cards then you have a chance at paying them down without still putting more purchases on them.

- Set some short term goals to keep you on track: While those long term goals can be really great, sometimes you need a few short term wins to keep you on track. These can help you see the benefits of going on the budget and can keep you motivated towards reaching those longer term goals. You could set a weekly food budget and stick with it. You could pick a smaller bill to pay off. You could decide to cut out how much you go out to eat for the month and stick with it. All of these are small goals, but they encourage you to stick with the diet plan and not fall off as easily.

There are a lot of great budgeting plans that you

can choose to use. All of them can be successful as long as they fit well with your budgeting plan and you are willing to not fall off them. Follow some of the tips above and you are sure to see how well the budget can work at saving you money and keeping you on track with your minimalistic budget.

Chapter 19:
Tips to Help You Cut Expenses Out of Your Budget

B udgeting is going to be different for everyone. It all depends on what you hold as the most important and what you value the most. You may decide that going out with friends every week is important so you want to adjust the budget to allow for this. But others may be just as happy with staying home and could cut this expense out. Minimalist budgeting is not all about getting rid of everything in your life but getting rid of the things that are just taking up space in your life and wasting your time and money.

There are a lot of things that you can do to make it easier to maintain your budget. And many things are just small little changes that you won't even notice after a few weeks. Some of the budgeting tips that seem small but quickly add up include:

- Cook a large meal. Pick something that doesn't spoil easy and that will fill you up. You can then use this for at least a few meals, and maybe some lunches in there as well, for less money. You can also consider doubling the recipe each time and freezing the second serving so you have extra for another night while only adding a few extra dollars total.

- Bring your own lunch to school or work.

- Do not head to the buffet at work or school to get your snacks. These are way higher in prices than going to a grocery store or making them on your own.

- Never go to the grocery store when you are hungry. Eat at least a snack before you go. When you go to the store when you are hungry, everything looks good and you will purchase more than you need.

- Write out a list before you head to the store and then stick to it. Don't veer off and try to avoid the sales boards or you may be tempted to purchase something that you don't need.

- Stick with the generic brands to get the most out of your money. They taste the same and work the same but can cost a lot less.

- Reuse your grocery bags. These often work well for tidying up the home and can save on trash bags.

- Pay all your bills early in the month so you don't end up paying any late fees.

- See if you are able to consolidate your debt payments with a lower interest rate to save you money.

- When it is time for a minimalist budget,

consider getting rid of your credit cards right away. If you are trying to pay off the credit card, consider finding one with a lower interest rate to help save you money.

- Get books that are used if you enjoy reading in your life or consider borrowing from the library so you don't have to buy anything.

- Set up an automatic savings account as we talked about before.

- If you ever get any extra money in your income, such as from a tax return, an inheritance, or a work bonus, don't go and spend it on something extra. Instead, use it to help you pay down some debts or use it to put into a savings account.

- Hold onto your loose change. This can be useful if you use the cash only method. Any time you make a purchase, take the change and put it to the side. You will be amazed at how much money you can save doing this and you can put that towards your budget or paying off some extra debts.

- Trade things in your family. If you know someone who needs a certain item that you have, ask them if they are willing to trade for one of their items.

- Set a price limit on any gifts that you give to friends and family. You don't want to do expensive gifts for Christmas or for your birthday. You don't want to go broke because of a holiday.

- Have a no spend day, no spend weekend,

or a no spend week. This is a time when you won't spend any money at all and if you can do it once or twice a month, can really help you out.

- Pair up with others when using different services like Spotify, Netflix and more. You can often add up to five people in the package and then you can divide up the costs.

- Instead of using a hotel when you travel, use an Airbnb, use Uber instead of Taxis, and search around to find the best deals on your traveling if you decide to do it.

- Buy summer clothes in the winter and then winter clothes in the summer. This can provide you with a huge discount. You could save 90 percent or more.

- Instead of spending a lot of money on entertainment, consider looking for any free events. There are often a lot of free events that you can choose to follow in your home town and this can keep you busy at night rather than going out and eating into your entertainment budget.

- Look at your bills each year: Don't just keep paying the same amount on your bills from one year to the next. You need to take the time to review them. You may find that there is a better deal going on for you, and it could save you a few hundred a year. Check your insurance, your cable, your phone, and other bills and see if you can get them for a better price each year.

- Have a date night at home: Having a date night can be expensive. You have to pay for a babysitter for the kids, pay to go out to eat, pay for a movie or any other entertainment that you enjoy. Instead of spending all that money, consider having a date night at home. You can make a meal, watch a movie, and even go for a romantic stroll without having to pay all that money.

- Cut the gym membership and use online videos: Many great programs are available online for you for free. Or there are more and more programs that move completely online and only require a small fee compared to the expensive gym membership.

- Be careful with the thermostat: Don't turn on the air conditioner too high or the heater either. These can be really expensive if you aren't careful. In the winter, put on more layers to keep you warm and in the summer, wear a little less or rely on fans to help you stay comfortable.

These are just a few of the tips that you can follow when it comes to keeping your budget in line. None of these are big changes in your life and you can implement them without much notice. But when you combine a few of them together, they can make a big difference in the amount of money that you spend. See which tips from above you are able to follow and add in some of your own and you are sure to get that budget in order and keep yourself on a minimalistic budget.

Conclusion

Many people are going to spend more money and time than they have on items that they don't really need. They will go out and purchase an item because they think they need it or because the advertisement was so powerful, or as a status symbol. They spend money that they don't have on the item and pull themselves further into debt than before. Then once that item is home, they run into trouble having to take care, maintain, and clean that item. This can rub salt in the wound because you have to worry about the debt that you have and the waste of time that cleaning that item entails.

The idea behind the lifestyle of minimalism, as well as on minimalistic budgeting, is that you need to get rid of anything that is taking up space and draining your budget. This idea is not meant to make you feel deprived or make you live with only a few items to your name. Many people mistake minimalism as poverty, as having nothing, but this can't be further from the truth.

As we talk about in this guidebook, there are many different ways to follow a minimalists lifestyle. You don't have to be broke to have this kind of lifestyle. And there are still plenty of people who spend their time traveling, enjoying nice things, and enjoying life who go on this kind of lifestyle. This is because minimalism is about getting rid of all the unnecessary junk, the stuff that we don't need and is just in the way and focusing more on keeping things that hold value to us, that make us happy and give us joy.

This can be a hard concept for many people. We have spent our whole lives learning that it is fine to just purchase everything. We take out longer loans on items, like cars, in order to make it fit into our budget, even though it really doesn't. We spend years in debt on items that aren't worth our time, on items that we don't need and that don't give us the happiness that we desire at all. And this can make us feel miserable.

This guidebook has taken some time to talk about minimalism budgeting. We spent some time discussing what minimalism is all about, some of the things that you need to be careful about when it comes to minimalism, and so much more. We also talked about the way that our minds work when we shop and when we hear advertisements and some of the things that you can do to fight against this unconscious battle between how the seller works on your brain and on how your know you should logically behave.

Then a good deal of your budget is going to focus on the different methods of budgeting that you can use. Each of these works well and it often depends on the method that you like and which one allows you to keep more of the things you love in your life. Some may be too restrictive when it comes to keeping the most important things around, so you may choose to pick something else for your budgeting needs.

Being minimalistic in your budget doesn't mean that you have to give up everything you hold dear. It is more about making a plan that allows you to get rid of the things that are just in the way and cluttering up your life and keep the things that bring you true happiness. This guidebook took the time to look more at minimalism and how it can be implemented in your budget so that you can stay out of debt while still enjoying the life that you love. Take a look inside this guidebook to help you get started with your new minimalist budget plan today!

About the Author

Mary Connor is a professional organizer, a wife and mom to three children, a cleaning expert, and a former finance manager. She is passionate about helping people lead better lives and shares easy and inexpensive organizing tips and tricks on how to clean up life's little and big messes. In addition, she teaches women how to pay off debts, improve their money management skills and increase their wealth.

In the past, Mary found her passion in writing and focuses on topics that can make a real difference in helping others accomplish their goals and dreams. She has made it a habit to continue learning new things so that she can share these insights with the world in a concise and helpful way. This interest has led her to the life of learning several factors affecting human interactions. Moreover, she continually works on expanding her knowledge by attending seminars and networking with other professionals.

Mary loves the outdoors and likes to walk or run every day. She is dedicated to the practice of mindfulness and feels that a minimalist lifestyle is important to both success and happiness. When not writing or walking, Mary enjoys spending time horseback riding with her daughters or relaxing at the lake with her husband.